The Essential Survival Guide for Cat Owners

-The Illustrated Dark Humor Companion
to Help You Understand Your Pet Kitten
and Why It Drives You Mad

Acknowledgements

To my boys, Ramses, Exit, and Bastian for making my life so totally impossible and wonderful at the same time.

To Elin at ZetunAB for convincing me that someone might enjoy my silly drawings.

To the Cornish Rex group on Facebook for being supportive beyond measure and sharing their cat stories with me! (https://www.facebook.com/groups/162672227143902/)

To Siw for being a sounding board and sometimes letting me work on the book instead of gaming with her...

The Essential Survival Guide for Cat Owners
–The Illustrated Dark Humor Companion to Help You Understand
Your Pet Kitten and Why It Drives You Mad

Published by Zetun AB / Zetun Förlag, Skövde, Sweden
www.zetun.se

Text © 2016 Mona Eklund
Illustrations © 2016 Mona Eklund
Cover art © 2016 Mona Eklund

Editor and Copyeditor Elin Rantakrans
Cover Design and Layout Elin Rantakrans
Proofreader Catherine Dewey

Printed 2016 in the EU
ISBN 978-91-980552-7-6

Thank you to Caroline B for letting me draw your Cornish Rex Roosta for the cover. And thank you Lisa B for letting me use the drawing of Squeegee to represent the Cornish Rex breed on page 25, and to Helen R and Sue R for letting me use a picture of two of your royal brood for reference on page 47.

The Essential Survival Guide for Cat Owners

–The Illustrated Dark Humor Companion
to Help You Understand Your Pet Kitten
and Why It Drives You Mad

About the author

I'm a crazy cat lady in training. I only have three cats, so I can't claim the title quite yet as I believe the lowest amount of cats you can have to proclaim yourself a Crazy Cat Lady (CCL) is seven.

I love telling strangers about my cats and hearing strangers tell me about theirs, so why not in book format? I also like to draw them, so this book is full of doodles, old and new.

Two of my cats are of the breed Cornish Rex and I apologize if this book is at all biased towards this breed... If you own a Rex yourself, I'm sure you understand. They have a specific look which generates a lot of comments:

Cat Tales

Someone saw my white Oatmeal on my porch and told me there was an albino possum there!
BEVERLY J

I'd been for a walk with Mailo. Met one of my neighbours with their very, very (VERY) loud Chihuahua. 10 meters away she said to her barking dog: 'Look over there, honey, there is another Chihuahua.' Mailo was so upset by being called 'a dog'.
MIR R

I let a little boy pat Pete at a cat show, and he said: 'He feels like my grandma's bed!'
SHEREE E

Introduction

Congratulations on purchasing this book. I will take a wild guess and say that you most likely share your life with a cat.

Not share *equally*, of course, cats have no concept of that, but you are most likely allowed to live in the same house. That's a good start.

The road to insanity begins with taking a first step, after all. This book will guide you through life with one or several cats. It will tell it as it is – be honest without sugarcoating anything – and give you all the advice you might need, except the number to a good therapist, which you might want to try to find on your own. The content of this book is based on hard earned experience along with in depth scientific research.

A word of caution – even though it seems designed for it, under no circumstances are you to throw this book at your cat. The cat might deserve it, but remember, you love your furry dictator.

WARNING:

Whut?

YOUR CAT WILL DO ANYTHING TO MAKE SURE YOU DON'T READ THIS BOOK.

ANYTHING.

Cat Tales

One night, my cat Darcy decided to investigate and leaped into my pot of chilli. I was washing dishes and tried to get her while my hands were dripping wet. When I did catch her and tried to clean her legs and body, I found out that red chilli stains don't come out of white fur very well. For the next week or two she resembled a tortoise with red feet and red spots on her belly and sides.   MARIETTE R

NOT RECOMMENDED USE BY THE AUTHOR.

A history of cats

Between 15 000 and 9 000 years ago it all went wrong – cats realized that humans could actually be very useful to them.

It is not completely clear what caused this insight, since this was before the can opener was invented, though it might have involved spilled milk and cuddles. Either way it was already too late to change fate. And making matters worse – the Egyptians decided to honor cats as gods, something cats still demand of us today. There have always been cat-atheists who have tried to change this trend, but cats are a resilient species; they have survived everything from witch hunts to the more common, *"just-look-what-the-damn-cat-did-to-the sofa"* calamities.

Unless you grew up with your cat, there are only two time-related terms you should be familiar with: *BC* and *AC*. That is the time before and after your cat came into your life.

THE FIRST LINE OF CAT ACTIVATION TOYS WAS
SHORT LIVED. SO WAS THE INVENTOR.

How to choose a kitten

This is one of the more pointless chapters of this book, simply because you won't take this advice.

First, remember that few people get their cat through careful planning and research. If this was the case, there would be a lot fewer of us with nervous tics and the acquired ability to hear just how much that crash from the other room just now will cost us. It's more common that the cat just suddenly appears and moves in – it seems to choose you. Or you get a call from a dear old friend who says you should come over and just look at their kittens.

Imagine that you get the opportunity to choose, and actually leave the house with the intention of picking out a furry little sociopath. You should choose a healthy, well-developed kitten whose temperament seems to match yours. Now, did you follow that advice? No, of course you didn't. You picked the smallest of the bunch, who threw itself from the cupboard, landed on your head for a moment, then made a splash into the aquarium, before landing at your feet where it looked up at you, cross eyed, as if it was all your fault. That's the one you picked to be your new life companion. No need to panic, because it actually doesn't matter if the kitten has a

—**Cat Tales**—

One year as my husband and I were walking around a cat show, we met an Abyssinia breeder who had two kittens for sale. As we were admiring them the little boy raised both of his paws up to my husband as if to say: 'Please pick me daddy!' Needless to say, we had our beloved Pogo for 18 years.   SUSAN C

pedigree longer than you, if it said hello calmly when you came to see it, ended up falling asleep in your lap, and has a clean bill of health from several vets – you're still in for it.

Remember that the cat you chose, or who chose you, is aware of the fine line between sanity and insanity; it will take you to the very edge but still manage to remain your sweetheart. Cats have made this balance into an art form.

QUIZ: WHICH OF THE KITTENS

ANSWER: THIS WAS, OF COURSE, A TRICK QUESTION,

ONE FROM THE LEFT

BELOW SHOULD YOU **NOT** PICK?

ALL WILL MAKE YOUR LIFE HELL. **B**UT THE SECOND IS AN ARSONIST.

Selected cat breeds

Trouble comes in many colors and body types. If you don't want to inherit a specific kind of problem and like the idea of being surprised, I recommend getting an ordinary domestic shorthaired cat.

Or perhaps a domestic longhaired cat for that matter, that is, a Moggy. You rarely know what you get with a Moggy, but they do seem to have a bit more common sense than many of the pure breeds. Be aware, however, that there is no such thing as *just a normal cat*. The cat is king, and it doesn't matter if you paid as much for it as for a small car, or if you found it in the gutter. Your cat will rule you and you will be grateful.

Contrary to the dog, the cat hasn't been bred for specific purposes, but only for their looks. Because there are humans with different levels of taste and intelligence some cat breeds have suffered, but hopefully intelligence will triumph over taste eventually.

If looks are not important to you, choose a cat based on its temperament. The spectrum goes from the Persian at one end to the Siamese at the other.

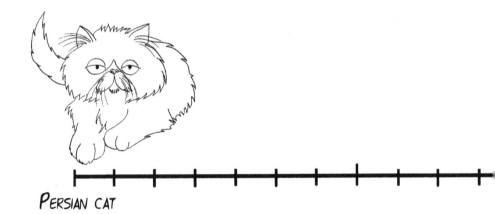

PERSIAN CAT

┌─Cat Tales─

My Shenzi loves my son's electric toothbrush. It makes it nearly impossible to brush his teeth without an audience, and he also has to show it to her before starting to brush.   RACHEL S

The ordinary domestic cat can be placed anywhere along this line but usually somewhere in the middle. The Persian is generally seen as calm and dignified, whereas the Siamese is lively and talkative.

Having a cat that will lie on the sofa and watch you with an almost ethereal calmness may seem ideal to most of us. But beware! Cats are planners. Revenge for baths or for buying the wrong brand of food might be weeks in the coming – but it will come. And it will be devastating.

The Siamese is a good actor to boot. It will loudly and with feeling tell the world about its opinions, thoughts, and deeds, usually all at once. Besides the breeds already mentioned the Moggy, the Persian, and the Siamese there are many, many others. Next follows a short presentation of a few of them.

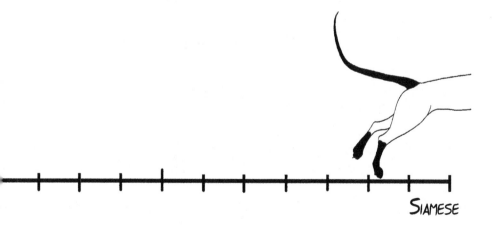

SIAMESE

The Bengal

If you don't think a regular cat is challenging enough, why not try one with actual wildcat ancestry? Bengals have the Asian Leopard cat in their genes (not to be confused with an actual leopard). The Bengal is not that dangerous. Probably. Actually, these beauties are bred to be very friendly, but that doesn't mean that they will not engage in mind games or pranks. These cats can jump like pros, are known to actually like water, need heaps of attention, and are playful. You'll be kept busy.

I'M A WILD THING!

─ **Cat Tales** ─

In the middle of the night my cat took my kid's marbles, hopped into the bath tub and played arcade ball. The noise would suddenly stop. A few minutes later it would start all over again. The next morning my daughter was taking her shower in the tub and the water wasn't draining. The cat had lifted up the drain and put the marbles in it. Try explaining that to your plumber. I told him the cat did it but he didn't believe me.   DEBBIE W M

The Birman

This cat is also called the "Sacred Cat of Burma", which doesn't exactly help them to come down to earth from their godlike status. A dazzling beauty with medium-long silky fur, it will look down its Roman nose at you and judge you with its sapphire blue eyes. Personality-wise the Birman is somewhere in the middle on the cat spectrum. Occasionally, it will let you make your own decisions, watching you with a laidback demeanor. And the next moment it will be in the middle of your project, making sure you are doing things right.

Cat Tales

We had a handyman at our house once. While he was crouched down working, my cat decided to jump on his back and watch what he was doing over his shoulder. I heard the man calling me from the other room saying 'Ma'am! Excuse me, ma'am! Can you please get your cat off my back'. Oops! Sorry!

LISA S

The British Shorthair

This breed can look deceivingly like a domestic shorthair to the untrained eye, but a clue is to look at their price tag. They are lovingly called "teddy bears" because of their thick, short fur and round cheeks. They have a sturdy build – though some are just fat – and an equally stubborn mind. They are a dignified breed, and aware that they have a pedigree. They put up with most things, but don't like to be carried around too much, mostly because they aren't handbags.

I'M NOT FAT.
YOU'RE FAT.

---**Cat Tales**---

Every time we had Mexican food, our cat would jump on the table and circle our plates as we wrapped our arms around them to protect our food. Thinking I would solve this problem, I got a really hot salsa, put it on a plate and let him taste it. That would teach him. The joke was on me... He loved it. DEBBIE W M

The Cornish Rex

Cornish Rex cats are born with big ears, a bad perm, a lanky body, and an inability to shut up. They would be the bully-victims of the cat world, but are far from it. However, they are an all-in-one circus: clown, acrobat, ringmaster, and elephant. How such graceful creatures can manage to be so clumsy is the next thing the *catologist* will have to look into. That is, after someone creates the title of catologist.

You simply can't overlook this breed. They won't let you. They demand your complete attention around the clock.

┌─**Cat Tales**────────────┐

Some kids walking past my house thought Nyne (my black smoke Cornish Rex) was a Halloween decoration. When he moved they screamed: 'Oh my god, it's alive!' and ran down the street.   TIFFANY M

The Devon Rex

Sometimes it is not easy to tell it apart from the Cornish Rex. Although, someone at some point in the history of this breed wanted something possibly even
more alien, slightly less bird-boned, friendlier to humans, and possibly even
clumsier than the Cornish Rex. A Devon Rex simply cannot exist without its
humans, but will agree to keep a watchful eye from the highest place available.
Some suspect they teleport up there.

WE CAME TO THIS
PLANET FOR FOOD AND
CUDDLES. SO GET TO IT.
HUMAN!

┌─Cat Tales─
My new cat, Cami,
leans forward, slowly,
adoringly towards my
face, gazing unblink-
ingly with her huge
yellow eyes. I am
entranced. With one
swift movement, she
lunges forward and
chomps down on my
left eyelashes with
unrestrained gusto.
She steps back lazily.
Looks very satisfied.
                NICOLE B

The Domestic cat

The Domestic Shorthair or Longhair, Moggie, or ordinary house cat is a cat with no pedigree but usually with a lot of common sense instead. A housecat can be loud... or quiet. Active... or still. Big... or small. Basically, you don't quite know what you get with a Moggie, but don't for a moment think that they are any *less* of a cat than a purebred. Underestimating any cat is a big mistake – you have to remember that they are all gods no matter how they came into your life and what their price tag was.

YEAH. I'VE BEEN WORKING ON IT ALL DAY. BUT THE CAT HAS BEEN BOTHERING ME.

NO. IT'S JUST AN ORDINARY CAT.

THE– THE CAT JUST WALKED OVER MY KEYBOARD AND FORMATTED MY HARD DRIVE! HOW THE HE–

"ORDINARY." HUH?

Cat Tales

My husband looked away for one minute, and Pete stole an entire rack of ribs off his plate and took off with it. The ribs were bigger than Pete!   SHEREE E

Just because you don't know my grandmother's name doesn't mean you don't have to peel shrimps for me, understand?

The Maine Coon

"Small children, small problems; big children, big problems," as the saying goes. This isn't true for cats – anyone who has had a kitten knows this – but if you want to prove the hypothesis, why not choose one of the biggest cat breeds around? The Maine Coon is a gentle giant, social and friendly, so you might ask what does it have up its sleeve? Well, for one thing the breed is known to chirp like birds. Mind tricks, I tell you. Mind tricks.

TWEET!

I DON'T TRUST
THAT NEW BIRD...

Cat Tales

Out of the mouth of babes. My three-year-old granddaughter introduced me to her curious playmates. 'Oh, this is my crazy cat Grandma', which produced an outburst of laughter from both sets of parents. I was speechless. JEANNINE R

I AM THE MAIN ATTRACTION

The Manx

Surprisingly, this cat is not from Sweden. You might think it was an IKEA model as its tail is usually missing – but no. It's supposed to look like that. Because its back legs are a bit longer than its front legs, it also walks a little funny. We try not to mention that. The breed stems from the Isle of Man, and they are known to be good hunters. Although very friendly and social towards their owners, they can be a bit shy towards strangers. Perhaps because they might be a little self-conscious about that walk.

<table>
<tr><td colspan="2">Cat Tales</td></tr>
<tr><td colspan="2">If forced to identify my kitty by a butthole line-up, I could locate Masha's no problem. I spend more time with her b-hole in my face than her actual face. Sigh.</td></tr>
<tr><td></td><td align="right">DEENAH B</td></tr>
</table>

The Ocicat

This is a cool cat in a tough packaging. This breed was named after the ocelot because of its spotted fur, but is thought to be friendly and loving despite its wild looks, meaning this cat has a good PR agency behind it. It actually doesn't have got any wildcat DNA at all. These cats love their toys and sometimes allow their owner to train them – mainly because they want attention. They usually aren't shy around guests or other pets; an Ocicat will be hanging around just to make sure they don't miss out on anything.

---**Cat Tales**---------------------------------

Our Banjo always enjoyed a good read except that he always ate the book corners, and sadly we let him.

CLAIRE AMANDA R

I'M ALWAYS SPOT ON

The Persian

The Persian cat is one of the oldest breeds, like the Siamese, but there the similarities end. The Persians are calmness personified. Some call them cushions, as they can be deceptively similar. This breed doesn't miss out on anything and they scheme. They are keen observers and, eventually, they will dish out any due punishment. Their long and fluffy coat demands some maintenance, which includes bathing now and then. Luckily, Persians tend to be quite accepting since it's beneath their dignity to throw a fit, unless it's really called for. They are less talkative than the loud Siamese, but when they have something to say it's usually important.

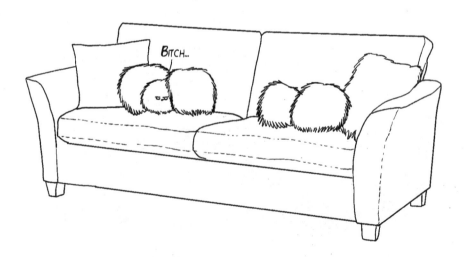

The Siamese

The Siamese is one of the oldest cat breeds in the world. They used to be held as holy cats by Thai monks. If this doesn't ring any warning bells you might want to reread this book a couple of times! Adding to the fact that they know they are extremely special and holy, they also talk. A lot. Their characteristic voice is low, demanding and difficult to disregard. They are very active and social, and they like a lot of company; both human and other cats. The Siamese comes with built in *masks* to disguise their true identity, something that also should be a warning sign... Still, if you want to be able to tell the most unbelievable cat stories to your friends then the Siamese might be the cat for you.

Cat Tales

My Siamese cat peed all over the computer of the insurance woman and then ruined her pantyhose. Why? She ignored my Siamese in the first place.

FEMKE F

THE SIAMESE IS PERFECT FOR DEALING WITH PHONE-SALESMEN.

The Ragdoll

Ragdolls tends to look like a mix of Persian and Birman, and that's more or less what they actually were from the very beginning. They belong to the giants of the cat world, which makes it easier for them to push you out of your bed at night. They have a rather relaxed attitude towards children, people in general, dogs, other cats, and anything else that might be considered annoying to most cats.

Cat Tales

My cats were seven years old when I married my husband. They knew they were there before him. One night we got in a terrible fight and I become very upset. My sweet cat Diego must have sensed how upset I was because he pooped inside my husband's shoe!   LORI L

The Russian Blue

Russians might not be known as the most romantic people in the world, but a more loving Russian than this is hard to find, at least if it belongs to you. These cats bond strongly to their owners but aren't always fond of guests. Or parties. Or change. Generally, they like routine and when everything is normal. They tend to choose a favorite human in a family and hang out with that person, demanding all the attention they feel they deserve – which is all of it.

Cat Tales

Years ago I was showing my beloved Bluie. I was rooming with a friend, and while I was in the bath, I could hear my friend laughing hysterically – she was watching Bluie play. She would sit up and with both paws hold the toy in her paws and shake it, then she'd get so excited at the stick she would let go with one paw and try and grab the toy itself, which would inevitably fall. She did this for two hours, sure she was going to eventually catch that elusive toy.   SALLY P

The Scottish Fold

We all tend to feel that our cats don't listen to us when we say something important like: "Let go of the roasted chicken!" This cat comes with ears ready to ignore every *"no"* it hears. This cat also tends to sit in weird positions, either up straight like a meerkat or slumped like a drunkard against the wall. They love their humans. They tend to hate being left alone for too long, which will make them sad, a heartbreaking sight in any cat, but even more so considering the ears of a typical Scottish Fold...

I'M SO HAPPY TO HAVE FINALLY FOUND A CAT THAT SUITS MY HUSBAND.

—Cat Tales—

I heard this loud crash, turned around and Super Cat passed me on the stairs. Dobby had climbed inside a plastic bag and stuck his head through the handle. It had scared him and he had started running through the house, with the bag attached looking like he was wearing a cape. TINA Q

The Sphynx

No one told the Sphynx in which line to stand to get fur, but fortunately, this enigmatic cat doesn't worry about this. After all, you pay for the heating in winter. The Sphynx belongs to the active side of the cat personality spectrum and can sometimes go far, far beyond what would be considered normal. Make sure to start drinking plenty of coffee so you can keep up. They love the spotlight and are always looking for a new audience. Strangers tend to become friends quickly. They also like to snuggle up for warmth, so having other cats or even dogs as companions is a good idea.

I'M WORRIED... I'VE BARELY SEEN PRINCESS SINCE WE GOT THE DOG... I DON'T THINK THEY LIKE EACH OTHER...

Cat Tales

I've had a builder's apprentice spot my cat, black smoke colour, and say: 'Oh my God, there's a devil cat!' SARA K

The cat's senses

The cat's five senses are not quite the same as a humans, as we shall see, though they are labelled the same.

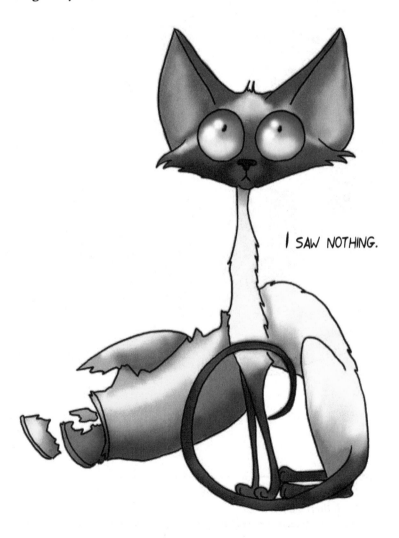

Selective hearing

A cat's ear is attached to no less than 32 individual muscles in order to make sure that your *"no!"* won't enter either of them. Cats in general seem to have a highly developed *selective hearing* ability, especially when it comes to what their humans might want. Flies, the sound of food canisters being opened, or something fun being dropped on the floor are things cats can hear from miles away.

20/20 vision

Cats are always watching. And judging. Maybe it's the way their eyes seem to glow in the dark or the fact that they don't have to blink as humans do that makes a cat's stare somewhat eerie. Just like with hearing cats also have *selective vision*, refusing to see the treat dropped in front of them if they don't think it has been done under the proper circumstances.

Cat Tales

Outside our apartment building is a playground. Once I overheard some children discussing if my Cornish Rex was a bat on our balcony, but one was sure it was a flying fox because he had seen one on TV.
RONJA A

I was having dinner but got up to see to something. When I returned Lilli was just as I had left her, lying next to my meal and a glass of wine. Everything was the same, except the glass was sideways and there was wine all over the table and dripping. But Lilli was still lying there staring at me.
LISA W

Distinct olfactory organs

A cat's sense of smell is much better than that of a human. Naturally, cats are better all around, aren't they? When it comes to smell they are about fourteen times better. This makes it impossible to bring roasted chicken into the house without it going unnoticed. Cats also mark their territories with smell, by rubbing against their property and, especially, with unneutered males, peeing on things. This makes rather little sense indoors and is hugely unpopular with the human members of the family.

Stingy touch

The cats' whiskers are their pride and joy – helping them to navigate in the dark, catch prey, and even signal their current mood. Mainly, they are used to tickle their owner's face early in the morning.

Cats use their paws to examine things, which is rather clever. Dogs, for example, mainly use their mouths, which causes them to be stung in the mouth by bees and wasps more often than cats, who are usually stung on their paws.

Cat Tales

My cat Zowie was a genius. At that time my significant other used to baby-sit her if I had to be somewhere, and one weekend she was at his house. Unbeknownst to me, my boyfriend was having an affair. During the night, he heard a small scuffle, but went back to sleep. In the morning the woman was running all over the flat trying to find her cosmetics. My boyfriend went into the kitchen. Zowie had gone into her suitcase, pulled out the cosmetics bag, dragged it into the kitchen, and dumped the whole thing into her giant water bowl. Ruined! All those expensive French cosmetics. Zowie laughed all the way home.   LISA W

Refined taste

The cat's sense of taste is very interesting. As a species cats lack the T1R2 protein, which makes it impossible for them to register sweet tastes. That, on their evolutionary journey, actually might be what made them into pure carnivores. If you can't taste the strawberries and whipped cream you're more likely to go for the barbecue. But that's not the interesting bit. What is interesting is how they can eat a stinkbug one minute only to refuse cuts of the finest beef the next.

SKY-RAISIN

SURELY YOU JEST?

---**Cat Tales**---
My cat tilts his heads to the sides if I'm eating something that he wants, and if I don't give it to him, a paw will come and try to grab it from me... Especially chips.
ALEKSANDRA B

The cat's metabolism

The stomach and intestines of a cat have developed in order to produce the maximum amount of nasty things with the smallest amount of intake.

Thankfully, most cats use a litter box without problems, mainly so they won't have to go out in the rain. Cats have discovered that by not dragging their owners out in rain and snow like dogs do, cat owners sometimes feel a little bit of gratitude towards them. The house might be a mess and ruled by a crazy tyrant, but at least they don't have to go out at 6 AM every morning in the storm.

The art of vomiting

Vomiting is one of the greater performances in a cat's repertoire. This art can be practiced anywhere at anytime and consist of anything: the prized house plant, the family's canary, the expensive cat food (see the chapter The cat's diet), or nothing at all. There are suspicions among cat owners that cats sometimes vomit simply because they can't think of anything else to do. Hairballs, something produced with pride by most felines, are considered perfect gifts for their owners.

The art of throwing up can be divided into two subcategories: *public* and *stealth vomiting*. Public vomiting is usually most common, as the cat saunters out into the middle of the room or to the closest light colored rug, and makes a few gagging noises to gain everyone's attention before proceeding to destroy the rug and everyone's appetite by retching loudly. The experienced cat owners have developed sensitized hearing and are ready to jump to pull away the rug, the shoes, the dog, or whatever the cat has set its sights on. It takes good reflexes, but cat owners develop these naturally over time.

---**Cat Tales**---

I had a cat named Kito. Once he caught a cockroach and ate it. A minute later he hacked it back up. When the cockroach came out, it stayed still for a second and then ran away. I screamed so loud the neighbours came to my door to see if I was okay!

LORI L

There is no defense, however, against the stealth vomits. These are usually conducted when no one is at home or everyone's asleep. The place chosen is never in the open but under beds, sofas, or other furniture that is rarely moved. The brown, dried piles are often found during a big cleaning spree or when the family is about to move out. At these times you can generally hear the culprit's pleased giggles in the background.

Some, often younger and inexperienced cats, sometimes just can't wait for the big revelation, and so try to point their owners to the scene of the crime prematurely. In most cases, however, the evidence has already dried, is as hard as cement, and can barely be removed without taking part of the flooring with it.

Urine and excrement

Normally, matters of the litterbox are handled nicely and discreetly. Perhaps with the exception of a stressed or unhappy cat that might "forget" the location of the litter box and its purpose.

Some cats like to tell their owners when they have visited the box and demand that it is cleaned immediately, even if their owner is busy entertaining guests. Well no, *especially* when the owner is busy entertaining guests. The cat displays its power, proving their humans simply to be marionettes in their claws by making them empty a smelly box in front of their visiting boss. This is while the cat now is sitting in said manager's lap, conversing politely about how hard it is to get any efficient help around the house these days.

Another activity well-known to most cat owners is the "poop-run". The cat comes out of the box looking weird, and starts to drag itself along the floor or simply dash around the house with poop trailing along behind it. This is often the human's fault, though, as the accidents are usually due to human hair mixed in with the excrement, creating some rather smelly and unattractive pearl necklaces. Again, quick reflexes are the only thing standing between the owner and utter destruction.

KEEP AT LEAST ONE BOX PER CAT. IN CASE OF EMERGENCIES.

The cat's diet

When the opportunity arises the cat is a picky eater – a gourmet. Though this doesn't necessarily mean the most expensive cat food on the market...

Gourmet food might be a half-rotten mouse or whatever is on your plate at the moment. It is impossible to give any general advice about food. Hopefully, your cat will accept a food brand that doesn't have to be imported from abroad and consist fully of the breast meat of quail... but it's not likely.

There are some rules to keep in mind:

The Amount Rule: You have bought a brand your cat loves. Next time you go shopping you fill up the cart with this brand. Result: your cat will never touch this food again.

The Adaption Rule: You take care of a cat that has had a tough life. It happily eats everything you serve it. You relax, wondering what all the fuss is about about feeding cats. Result: two weeks later you are sobbing into your morning coffee, surrounded by exclusive and very expensive cat foods while your beloved cat refuses to eat anything but cheese spread and crispy bacon – from your plate.

The Serving Rule: Cats do not always eat when food is served. This is normal and shouldn't be interpreted as the food having gone bad. Nervous cat owners tend to think

─────**Cat Tales**─────
I had a brilliant black half-Siamese named Comet. One morning I found a mouse in the kitchen. It was completely inside out!   LISA W

that their darlings will starve to death. Result: the food circus commences. One reason cats don't eat immediately is: "Let's see if something better comes along".

The Broken Bowl Rule: If a bowl is not filled up properly so that the bottom of it can't be seen, then it must be broken, and thus no food will be eaten from it until the bottom is covered once more. This is especially important if it's a bowl of dry food and it's three o'clock in the morning.

Liquids

A cat should always have clean, fresh water available. You simply have to over-look the fact that the cat is more likely to drink from the toilet or from the bath-room floor after you've taken a shower.

Milk should be avoided, as most cats are lactose intolerant after they've stopped nursing. If your cat has made it its life goal to get any milk or cream, which might exist in the house, you are in for lifelong defensive warfare. This would result in smelly litter boxes whenever you let your guard down. Look at it like a game, it's fun. Try to tell yourself that.

> ┌─**Cat Tales**─────────────────────────
> *I have a boy that only drinks water off his paw. Dip, lap, dip, lap, dip, lap.*
> MAGGIE E C

Suitable and unsuitable food

Just as we can't let small children decide their own diet, we can't let our cats dictate the rules when it comes to what they eat. They need a balanced diet where the energy intake is adjusted according to their individual needs. If anyone reading this is ever successful in that endeavor, please share. The rest of us would like to find out how you did it. A large part of cats' diet consists of things they should not eat, and which can be dangerous for them such as potted plants, bugs, and pieces of string. It is hard to stop your cat from trying different treats like these, even though many cat owners go through their homes like detectives. Despite this effort it's not unusual to see a cat throwing up Christmas tree tinsel in July.

Feline behaviors

All cats display some peculiar behaviors at times. These behaviors are what make them cats. Some are odder than others.

Things around your house will gradually start belonging to your cat: the *cat's* chair, the *cat's* side of the bed, the *cat's* blankets. All of these used to be *your* favorites. No place in your house is safe, which is something you should carefully consider. Your cat needs at least one indoor clawing post or climbing tree. These are always appreciated. In fact, the only reason your cat claws on the sofa is because they want their beloved clawing post to last for as long as possible.

I HAVE A GOOD BED. AND STILL I OFTEN WAKE UP WITH BACK PAINS...

...I WONDER WHY?

---**Cat Tales**---

Every night at 9:45 Mookie would tell me it's time for bed. Didn't matter where we were or if I was busy. She now does the same thing for her owner. And just like me he follows directions!

LINDA J

The sophisticated hunter

All cats hunt. Even in their sleep. It makes no difference whether your cat has been unable to catch a dust bunny, or if it regularly drops adders and badgers at your doorstep; all cats are *great* hunters. Try not to laugh at them too much when they fail – at least not to their faces. Some cats hunt from above, throwing themselves into the great abyss to catch an imaginary fly only to land on your head. Some are sneakier and hide underneath things, attacking any mouse, bug, or ankle, which might wander by. All cats dream of one day catching that *red dot* – a legend in the cat world. The elusive red dot, known to us humans as a laser pointer, is a great way to activate most cats.

Funny games

Cats like getting toys. It's not the object itself that is important. The cat might never look much at it, but because of their divine history your cat knows it is entitled to votive offerings.

How long a cat plays with something often stands in direct relation to how expensive or inappropriate the toy is; the more expensive the less play time. The more dangerous, like a snake, or valuable, like a diamond earring, and the game can go on for hours. The diamond earring will then carefully be deposited in a crack between the floor and the skirting board not to reappear until that strange metal sound from the vacuum cleaner tells you that you have to dig through pounds of dirt just in case it wasn't a thumbtack. The snake, or parts of it, will, with no exception, end up in your bed.

Cardboard boxes and paper bags are something that cats go crazy about. They are most interested in things that are not meant for them. But if you make the mistake of cutting a door and a window in the cardboard box, or cut away the handles of the bags so the cat won't get stuck, its interest immediately vanishes.

A crumpled piece of paper is a favorite toy of many cats. The worst thing you can do is to try to impress it with delicately folded origami creations. The most important rule when it comes to toys is to not seem insistent or enthusiastic. Then your cat will look at you like you're an idiot and leave the room.

The funny sound game is a game where the cat pushes things onto the floor as a way to get back at humans. It is purely scientific as the feline species is compiling a study of the different sounds things make when they hit the floor. You might think that by now they should know what sound a glass hitting the floor makes, but then again you are just a silly human.

The thieving game. There is no use denying it – cats are thieves. One might go as far as calling them kleptomaniacs. They can be sneaky about it, leaving you to wonder where a piece of jewelery or an odd sock went, or they can be as bold as anything. Somehow, taking things that aren't theirs seem to be within their rights as felines. Dogs retrieve. Cats taketh away.

Cat Tales

My first kitty was a Sphynx nicknamed 'Sir Pudge'. I always said he was my second in command as he was very protective of me. Once I had to shout at one of our greyhounds to lie down on the dog bed, as he'd been whining for a while. A couple of minutes later 'Sir Pudge' waddled out of the bedroom down the hall, where his favourite bed was kept. As I watched, he went over to the now quiet greyhound, swapped him on the snout and waddled back down the hall. The dog looked over at me like: 'What the hell just happened?' 'Sir Pudge' clearly was supporting my ruling – just in his own sweet, chubby time. FRAN M

WHAT ARE YOU HOLLERING ABOUT? IT'S NOT LIKE I'M HIDING...

Hide and Seek is another favorite game of many cats. Some cats will claim that they don't play this game intentionally, but they would be lying. Many cat owners' panic attacks could have been avoided if the cat would simply speak up when called or at least move. It ought to be impossible to lose three cats in a one-bedroom apartment for a good half hour, but all while the cats are silently snickering at their human's panic and agony.

A cat owner can look in a room and often immediately tell what the cat has done to it, but at the same time find it impossible to spot the cat itself. Some believe that cats have an ability to turn invisible, however, this is something they occasionally forget to turn off. This leads to their human desperately searching for the cat all through the house, several times, while the cat is watching from its place on full display on the sofa.

Traveling with your cat

Don't.

Sometimes you have to travel with them, like to the vet. Make sure to have a secure transport cage. The definition of secure is that a full-grown man with a sledgehammer shouldn't be able to get out. Then secure it with some chains and a padlock. Make sure you only have a travel time of 10 minutes maximum.

Body language

If you think that cats are unpredictable you need to think again. And learn to read their body language.

There are people who like dogs better than cats simply because they claim cats are *unpredictable*. Well, cats can be, of course, but mostly it'is because cats aren't really that interested in communicating with us humans, unless it's about something important, like dinner being late.

Dogs are pack animals and therefore very interested in understanding others as well as making themselves understood. They do everything to the point of holding up signs. Cats believe you just ought to know what you have done wrong and if you don't get the hint then you'll have to pay.

Cats don't need to understand us two-legged-cats. Point out something to a dog and the dog will most likely look in that direction. A cat will look at your finger wondering what the heck you're on about. This, however, doesn't mean that cats are stupid or anti-social. Cats have simply developed the language skills they need, and are very well adapted to communicating with their special human, if not with humans in general. Cats also greet their humans in a quieter, more dignified way than dogs, as a cat might just *happen* to brush up against your legs or blink at you from its resting spot.

Visual dictionary:

Ears: One of the best ways to check for a cat's mood is checking its ears. All emotions from happy to "I will murder you" are displayed there.

Tail and fur: A whipping tail means danger to everyone and everything around, and it usually starts with the tip twisting more and more. Watch out. Cats try to make themselves look bigger by having their fur stand on end, which is especially noticeable on the tail. This doesn't always occur when the cat is in a bad mood; the cat may simply be playing. The look makes it hard not to laugh, especially with kittens. But don't. Oh dear, don't. They will remember.

Whiskers: The whiskers spread out pointing forwards is a good sign, unless you're a mouse or other possible prey. Cats that are tired or grumpy can have their whiskers collected and folded back against their cheeks.

Eyes: Most cat owners know about *the slow blink*, which is how a cat is said to smile. Feel free to blink back, the cat already thinks you're a bit of a weirdo. However, simply staring at a cat is very rude, but then again so is staring at humans. Something cats don't care about, of course.

Paws: *Here be claws.* Here should be claws; in a few places in the world it's still legal to declaw a cat, but thankfully these places are getting fewer and fewer. It's illegal in around 24 countries since it's considered cruelty against animals.

---**Cat Tales**-------------------------------

My cat Mocca once caught a mouse, brought it inside and then let it go. It ended up living behind my fridge for a week. I could see and hear it, but apparently, according to Mocca, it was now my problem, not his.　　　　　　　　　　　　　SIW S

If you don't want to have a cat without amputating its claws, I strongly suggest you get a goldfish instead.

The claws are not only used to check the durability of the new couch, they are also used to climb, mark territories, hunt, and to some extent to groom. And they clearly help the human understand that moving right now isn't appreciated, as the cat just got comfortable in your lap.

Paws are also for kneading, an instinctual behavior the kitten uses to get the milk bar to work better, but which the adult cat continues with to show it's appreciation during a really nice cuddle session or for a particularly soft blanket.

---Cat Tales---
One day our cat Scully was tossing this long skinny toy up into the air multiple times with complete abandon. I didn't remember her ever having such a skinny toy. Then, to my horror, it dawned on me. What she was so gleefully tossing around was one of our lizards. The mesh top on the terrarium had been pushed in and she had taken out the lizard for her enjoyment. The lizard was miraculously unhurt! LINDSEY O

Vocal dictionary

Most cats have a large vocabulary that every cat owner does their best to figure out. Below follows a short list of translations:

Harmony and peace: A calm/happy purring. The cat is at ease and any owner knows to appreciate this sound and learn not to disturb the cat at this point. Not even if the cat is curled up on a body part that has fallen asleep.

Disharmony and annoyance: Intense/annoyed purring. This is the more intense sound, which the calm/happy purring turns into if whatever the cat is lying on decides to move. As a warning it is usually accompanied by one or two claws pressed against the skin.

I am hungry: An insistent short call or a long complaining cry, depending on if the cat is politely reminding you that it's dinner time or if it is dying of starvation. Often only seconds pass between these instances. The well-trained human moves quickly.

Let me in/out: An intensely pleading or demanding sound. If it is not obeyed, a wide range of vengeful actions might follow it. It is not only used to get outside; any form of door instantly leads to the cat wanting to be on the other side of it. This often ends with the cat being shut in somewhere, so the *let-me-in-sound* is usually instantly followed by a *let-me-out-cry*.

I'm feeling very romantic right now: A sound which usually only owners of cats who haven't been neutered ever hear. Might require some tranquilizer… for the owner.

Here I come: A short, almost bird-like sound, which polite cats use to warn that they now intend to sit on you.

And then he said, and then I said: Conversation sounds can vary indefinitely, but pay attention to the endnote. If it lowers into a sad *meeeuuw*, it's likely that the story has a tragic ending like the fly getting away. If it ends with a high note it most likely means that the vase made a funny noise when it hit the floor.

The growling monster: Even the smallest kitten can sometimes sound like a lion, or at least the stomach of a lion when it has a hankering for zebra.

This may stem from the cat being royally pissed off, but it might also just come from playing, as the cat uses its imagination and pretends that it's *The Great Hunter* (see the section on hunting). Pretend to be impressed in either case.

Oh, cruel world: Common when you have to take the cat for a car ride. Try not to stop anywhere along the road or people nearby will call the police reporting a kidnapping.

The cats and their owners

It is practically impossible for cat owners not to talk about their cat, and there is a really good reason for this – therapists are expensive.

When cat owners meet they talk about what the latest disaster cost them, be it in monetary value or gray hairs. When dog owners come together they try to topple each other with stories about how well trained their dogs are. We cat owners

MY HUMAN COMPLAINS WHEN I WAKE HER UP, BUT GETS UP AT ONCE WHEN THAT BOX ON HER NIGHT STAND STARTS MAKING NOISES... PLEASE EXPLAIN?

MY HUMAN JUST CAN'T LEARN THE EXACT RIGHT AMOUNT OF BELLY RUBS. THERE'S ALWAYS TOO MANY OR TOO FEW.

I LOVE TO SLEEP CURLED UP UNDER MY HUMAN'S CHIN. I DON'T CARE HOW HE LIKES TO SLEEP.

MY HUMAN COMPLAINS ABOUT CARRYING IN ALL THOSE BAGS OF FOOD, BUT COMPLAINS EVEN MORE WHEN I CARRY IN MY OWN... WHAT DO HUMANS HAVE AGAINST MICE?

need this therapy talk. We need to know that there are others in the same situation as us out there, who put up with getting tormented by little soft, cute, dictators who really (according to cat-atheists) shouldn't have a say in anything. Non-cat people, even if they like cats in general, think us weird. That's okay. They don't understand. They don't know. No matter how much the cats use us, they will always be on our side when it counts.

Conclusion

Cat people are not crazy. We're not. Yes, this book seems to prove the opposite, but the cats made us this way. We just like the unpredictable.

One might argue that having cats in the first place might be a sign of insanity. Well, maybe it is. But if having cats is crazy, I for one don't want to be sane. High blood pressure? Pet a cat! There's no better way to relax after a long day of trying to prevent catastrophes. Cat owners have lightning fast reflexes, we think on our feet, and always have new weird stories to share, and an almost supernatural ability to sense when something is wrong.

When new cats come into our lives we are always somewhat surprised that we, yet again, find ourselves adapting to weird unwritten rules and little quirks of the new Master. Some cat owners pretend that they don't submit at all, but just dig a little deeper and they will break down, admit to peeling and slicing shrimps on Friday nights or sleeping with just one pillow nowadays, as the cat *has* to sleep on the other. But you know what? It's okay. We're here for each other. We understand. When you go to bed tonight, with a cold cat nose stuck in your ear, purring so your skull is vibrating, then know that you are not alone. And remember that, in fact... you're lucky!

RUB MY BELLY, HUMAN...

BUT ONLY FOUR TIMES!

THERE WAS SUPPOSED TO BE A CAT HERE,
BUT IT LEFT.

Lightning Source UK Ltd.
Milton Keynes UK
UKOW06n2240030217
293540UK00002B/2/P